W9-ABS-723

THE FUNCTION OF REASON

THE FUNCTION OF REASON

By Alfred North Whitehead

Beacon Press   Boston

Copyright 1929 by Princeton University Press

First Beacon Paperback edition published in 1958 by arrangement
with the Princeton University Press

Printed in the United States of America

Beacon Press books are published under the auspices
of the Unitarian Universalist Association
This book is comprised of the Louis Clark Vanuxem Foundation
Lectures delivered at Princeton University, March 1929
International Standard Book Number: 0–8070–1573–3

9

INTRODUCTORY SUMMARY

History discloses two main tendencies in the course of events. One tendency is exemplified in the slow decay of physical nature. With stealthy inevitableness, there is degradation of energy. The sources of activity sink downward and downward. Their very matter wastes. The other tendency is exemplified by the yearly renewal of nature in the spring, and by the upward course of biological evolution. In these pages I consider Reason in its relation to these contrasted aspects of history. Reason is the self-discipline of the originative element in history. Apart from the operations of Reason, this element is anarchic.

CHAPTER ONE

CHAPTER ONE

The topic here considered—The Function of Reason—is one of the oldest topics for philosophical discussion. What is the function of Reason amid the welter of our mental experiences, amid our intuitions, our emotions, our purposes, our decisions of emphasis? In order to answer such a question we have to consider the nature of Reason, its essence. Of course this is a hackneyed theme. Its discussion stretches back to the very beginnings of philosophic thought. But it is the business of philosophers to discuss such fundamental topics, and to set them on the stage illuminated by our modern ways of thinking.

Various phrases suggest themselves, which recall the special controversies depending upon the determination of the true function of Reason:

Faith and Reason: Reason and Authority: Reason and Intuition: Criticism and Imagination: Reason, Agency, Purpose: Scientific Methodology: Philosophy and the Sciences: Rationalism, Scepticism, Dogmatism: Reason and Empiricism: Pragmatism.

Each of these phrases suggests the scope of Reason, and the limitation of that scope. Also the variety of topics included in them shows that we shall not exhaust our subject by the help of a neat little verbal phrase.

Yet in despite of this warning to avoid a mere phrase, I will start with a preliminary definition of the function of Reason, a definition to be illustrated, distorted, and enlarged, as this discussion proceeds.

The function of Reason is to promote the art of life.

In the interpretation of this definition, I must at once join issue with the evolutionist fallacy suggested by the phrase "the survival of the fittest." The fallacy does not consist in believing that in the struggle for existence the fittest to survive eliminate the less fit. The fact is obvious and stares us in the face. The fallacy is the belief that fitness for survival is identical with the best exemplification of the Art of Life.

In fact life itself is comparatively deficient in survival value. The art of persistence is to be dead. Only inorganic things persist for great lengths of time. A rock survives for eight hundred million years; whereas the limit for a tree is about a thousand years, for a man or an elephant about fifty or one hundred years, for a dog about twelve years, for an insect about one year. The problem set by the doctrine of evolution is to explain how complex organisms with such deficient survival power ever evolved. They certainly did not appear because they were better at that game than the rocks around them. It may be possible to explain "the origin of species" by the doctrine of the struggle for existence among such organisms. But certainly this struggle throws no light whatever upon the emergence of such a general type of complex organism, with faint survival power. This problem is not to be solved by any dogma, which is the product of mere abstract thought elaborating its notions of the fitness of things. The solution requires that thought pay full attention to the empirical evidence, and to the whole of that evidence.

The range of species of living things is very large. It stretches from mankind throughout all the vertebrates, and the insects, and the barely organized animals which seem like societies of cells, and throughout the varieties of vegetable life, and down to the minutest microscopic forms of life. At the lower end of the scale, it is hazardous to draw any sharp distinction between living things and inorganic matter. There are two ways of surveying this range of species. One way abstracts from time, and considers the variety of species as illustrating various levels of life. The other way emphasizes time, by considering the genetic relations of the species one to another.

The latter way embraces the doctrine of evolution, and interprets the vanishing of species and of sporadically variant individuals, as being due to maladjustment to the environment. This explanation has its measure of truth: it is one of the great generalizations of science. But enthusiasts have so strained its interpretation as to make it explain nothing, by reason of the fact that it explains everything. We hardly ever know the definite character of the struggle which occasioned the disappearance. The phrase is like the liturgical refrain of a litany, chanted over the fossils of vanished species. If the mere fact of dying out be sufficient proof of maladjustment to the environment, the explanation is reduced to a tautology. The importance of the doctrine of the struggle for existence depends on the assumption that living beings reproduce themselves in sufficient numbers of healthy offspring, and that adaptation to the environment is therefore the only decisive factor. This double assumption of prolificness and of healthiness is obviously not always true in particular instances. There are limitations to the doctrine of Malthus.

But there is another factor in evolution which is not in the least explained by the doctrine of the survival of the fittest. Why has the trend of evolution been upwards? The fact that organic species have been produced from inorganic distributions of matter, and the fact that in the lapse of time organic species of higher and higher types have evolved are not in the least explained by any doctrine of adaptation to the environment, or of struggle.

In fact the upward trend has been accompanied by a growth of the converse relation. Animals have progressively undertaken the task of adapting the environment to themselves. They have built nests, and social dwelling-places of great complexity; beavers have cut down trees and dammed rivers; insects have elaborated a high community life with a variety of reactions upon the environment.

Even the more intimate actions of animals are activities modifying the environment. The simplest living things let their food swim into them. The higher animals chase their food, catch it, and masticate it. In so acting, they are transforming the environment for their own purposes. Some animals dig for their food, others stalk their prey. Of course all these operations are meant by the common doctrine of adaptation to the environment. But they are very inadequately expressed by that statement; and the real facts easily drop out of sight under cover of that statement. The higher forms of life are actively engaged in modifying their environment. In the case of mankind this active attack on the environment is the most prominent fact in his existence.

I now state the thesis that the explanation of this active attack on the environment is a three-fold urge: (i) to live, (ii) to live well, (iii) to live better. In fact the art of life is *first* to be alive, *secondly* to be alive in a satisfactory way, and *thirdly* to acquire an increase in satisfaction. It is at this point of our argument that we have to recur to the function of Reason, namely the promotion of the art of life. The primary function of Reason is the direction of the attack on the environment.

This conclusion amounts to the thesis that Reason is a factor in experience which directs and criticizes the urge towards the attainment of an end realized in imagination but not in fact.

From the point of view of prevalent physiological doctrine this thesis is a complete heresy. To the older discussions mentioned earlier—Faith and Reason, Reason and Authority, and so on—I should have added one other, Physiology and Final Causation. When we have added that item, we have placed the discussion of Reason in its modern setting.

In fact we have now before us the two contrasted ways of considering Reason. We can think of it as one among the operations involved in the existence of an animal body, and we can think of it in abstraction from any particular animal operations. In this latter mode of consideration, Reason is the operation of theoretical realization. In theoretical realization the Universe, or at least factors in it, are understood in their character of exemplifying a theoretical system. Reason realizes the possibility of some complex form of definiteness, and concurrently understands the world as, in one of its factors, exemplifying that form of definiteness.

The older controversies have mainly to do with this latter mode of considering Reason. For them, Reason is the godlike faculty which surveys, judges and understands. In the newer controversy Reason is one of the items of operation implicated in the welter of the process. It is obvious that the two points of view must be brought together, if the theoretical Reason is to be satisfied as to its own status. But much confusion is occasioned by inconsistently wavering between the two standpoints without any coordination of them. There is Reason, asserting itself as above the world, and there is Reason as one of many factors within the world. The Greeks have bequeathed to us two figures, whose real or mythical lives conform to these two notions— Plato and Ulysses. The one shares Reason with the Gods, the other shares it with the foxes.

We can combine the discussion of these two aspects of Reason by considering the relevance of the notion of final causation to the behaviour of animal bodies. We shall then see how the theoretical and practical Reason in fact operate in the minds of men.

Those physiologists who voice the common opinion of their laboratories, tell us with practical unanimity that no consideration of final causes should be allowed to intrude into the science of physiology. In this respect physiologists are at one with Francis Bacon at the beginning of the scientific epoch, and also with the practice of all the natural sciences.

In this rejection of final causation the testimony seems overwhelming, until we remember that it is testimony of exactly the same force and character as that which led the educated section of the classical world to reject the Christian outlook, and as that which led the educated scholastic world to reject the novel scientific outlook of the sixteenth and seventeenth centuries. We have got to remember the two aspects of Reason, the Reason of Plato and the Reason of Ulysses, Reason as seeking a complete understanding and Reason as seeking an immediate method of action.

As a question of scientific methodology there can be no doubt that the scientists have been right. But we have to discriminate between the weight to be given to scientific opinion in the selection of its methods, and its trustworthiness in formulating judgments of the understanding. The slightest scrutiny of the history of natural science shows that current scientific opinion is nearly infallible in the former case, and is invariably wrong in the latter case. The man with a method good for purposes of his dominant interests, is a pathological case in respect to his wider judgment on the coordination of this method with a more complete experience. Priests and scientists, statesmen and men of business, philosophers and mathematicians, are all alike in this respect. We all start by being empiricists. But our empiricism is confined within our immediate interests. The more clearly we grasp the intellectual analysis of a way regulating procedure for the sake of those interests, the more decidedly we reject the inclusion of evidence which refuses to be immediately harmonized with the method before us. Some of the major disasters of mankind have been produced by the narrowness of men with a good methodology. Ulysses has no use for Plato, and the bones of his companions are strewn on many a reef and many an isle.

The particular doctrine in question is, that in the transformations of matter and energy which constitute the activities of an animal body no principles can be discerned other than those which govern the activities of inorganic matter. There can be no dispute as to the main physiological facts. No reactions between the material components of an animal body have been observed which in any way infringe the physical and chemical laws applying to the behavior of inorganic material. But this is a very different proposition from the doctrine that no additional principles can be involved. The two propositions are only identical on the supposition that the sort of physical principles involved are sufficient to determine definitely the particular activities of each physical body.

This is certainly not the case if we refer to principles such as the conservation of energy, and the chemical reactions. It is often assumed that even the one law of the conservation of energy determines without ambiguity the activities to which it applies. It is difficult to undertand how such a baseless fiction could have arisen.

But the point to which I wish to draw attention is the mass of evidence lying outside the physiological method which is simply ignored in the prevalent scientific doctrine. The conduct of human affairs is entirely dominated by our recognition of foresight determining purpose, and purpose issuing in conduct. Almost every sentence we utter and every judgment we form, presuppose our unfailing experience of this element in life. The evidence is so overwhelming, the belief so unquestioning, the evidence of language so decisive, that it is difficult to know where to begin in demonstrating it. For example, we speak of the policy of a statesman or of a business corporation. Cut out the notion of final causation, and the word "policy" has lost its meaning. As I write this lecture, I intend to deliver it in Princeton University. Cut out the notion of final causation, and this "intention" is without meaning. Again consider the voyage of the battleship *Utah* round the South American continent. Consider first the ship itself. We are asked to believe that the concourse of atoms, of iron, and of nitrogen, and of other sorts of chemical elements, into the form of the ship, of its armour, of its guns, of its engines, of its ammunition, of its stores of food,—that this concourse was purely the outcome of the same physical laws by which the ocean waves aimlessly beat on the coasts of Maine. There could be no more *aim* in one episode than in the other. The activity of the shipbuilders was merely analogous to the rolling of the shingle on the beach.

Pass on now to consider—still presupposing the orthodox physiological doctrine—the voyage of the ship. The President-elect of the United States had nothing to do with it. His intentions with respect to South American policy and goodwill in the world were beside the question, being futile irrelevancies. The motions of his body, those of the bodies of the sailors, like the motions of the shipbuilders, were purely governed by the physical laws which lead a stone to roll down a slope and water to boil. The very idea is ridiculous.

We shall of course be told that the doctrine is not meant to apply to the conduct of men. Yet the bodily motions are physiological operations. If these latter be blind, so are the motions. Also men are animals. Surely, the whole fight over evolution was about this very latter point.

Again we are told that we should look at the matter historically. Mankind has gradually developed from the lowliest forms of life, and must therefore be explained in terms applicable to all such forms. But why construe the later forms by analogy to the earlier forms. Why not reverse the process? It would seem to be more sensible, more truly empirical, to allow each living species to make its own contribution to the demonstration of factors inherent in living things.

I need not continue the discussion. The case is too clear for elaboration. Yet the trained body of physiologists under the influence of the ideas germane to their successful methodology entirely ignore the whole mass of adverse evidence. We have here a colossal example of anti-empirical dogmatism arising from a successful methodology. Evidence which lies outside the method simply does not count.

We are, of course, reminded that the neglect of this evidence arises from the fact that it lies outside the scope of the methodology of the science. That method consists in tracing the persistence of the physical and chemical principles throughout physiological operations.

The brilliant success of this method is admitted. But you cannot limit a problem by reason of a method of attack. The problem is to understand the operations of an animal body. There is clear evidence that certain operations of certain animal bodies depend upon the foresight of an end and the purpose to attain it. It is no solution of the problem to ignore this evidence because other operations have been explained in terms of physical and chemical laws. The existence of a problem is not even acknowledged. It is vehemently denied. Many a scientist has patiently designed experiments for the *purpose* of substantiating his belief that animal operations are motivated by no purposes. He has perhaps spent his spare time in writing articles to prove that human beings are as other animals so that "purpose" is a category irrelevant for the explanation of their bodily activities, his own activities included. Scientists animated by the purpose of proving that they are purposeless constitute an interesting subject for study.

Another reason for the extrusion of final causation is that it introduces a dangerous mode of facile explanation. This is certainly true. The laborious work of tracing the sequence in physical antecedents is apt to be discouraged by the facile suggestion of a final cause. Yet the mere fact that the introduction of the notion of final causation has its dangers is no reason for ignoring a real problem. Even if heads be weak, the problem remains.

The Christian clergy have often brought forward the same objections to innovations judged dangerous to faith and morals. The scientific world vehemently resents such limitations to the free consideration of evidence. Yet in defence of their own dogmas, the scientists act no otherwise than do the clergy. The physiologists and the legislature of the State of Tennessee exhibit the same principles of human conduct. In fact all types of men are on a level in this respect, and we shall never improve unless we understand the source of our temptation.

The evolution of Reason from below has been entirely pragmatic, with a short range of forecast. The primitive deep-seated satisfaction derived from Reason, a satisfaction arising out of an immemorial heredity, is provided by the emphatic clarification of some method regulating current practice. The method works and Reason is satisfied. There is no interest beyond the scope of the method. Indeed this last statement is too restrained. There is active interest restraining curiosity within the scope of the method. Any defeat of that interest arouses an emotional resentment. Empiricism vanishes.

The best chance for the wider survey is that it also should present itself with the promise of a wider method. Sometimes the reigning method is already showing signs of exhaustion. The main evidence that a methodology is worn out comes when progress within it no longer deals with main issues. There is a final epoch of endless wrangling over minor questions.

Each methodology has its own life history. It starts as a dodge facilitating the accomplishment of some nascent urge of life. In its prime, it represents some wide coordination of thought and action whereby this urge expresses itself as a major satisfaction of existence. Finally it enters upon the lassitude of old age, its second childhood. The larger contrasts attainable within the scope of the method have been explored and familiarized. The satisfaction from repetition has faded away. Life then faces the last alternatives in which its fate depends.

These last alternatives arise from the character of the three-fold urge which I have already mentioned: To live, to live well, to live better. The birth of a methodology is in its essence the discovery of a dodge to live. In its prime it satisfies the immediate conditions for the good life. But the good life is unstable: the law of fatigue is inexorable. When any methodology of life has exhausted the novelties within its scope and played upon them up to the incoming of fatigue, one final decision determines the fate of a species. It can stabilize itself, and relapse so as to live; or it can shake itself free, and enter upon the adventure of living better.

In the latter event, the species seizes upon one of the nascent methodologies concealed in the welter of miscellaneous experience beyond the scope of the old dominant way. If the choice be happy, evolution has taken an upward trend: if unhappy, the oblivion of time covers the vestiges of a vanished race.

With a happy choice, the new method quickly reaches its meridian stage. There is thus a new form of the good life, with its prolongation depending on the variety of contrast included within its methodical scope. On the whole, the evidence points to a certain speed of evolution from a nascent methodology into the middle stage which is relatively prolonged.

In the former event, when the species refuses adventure, there is relapse into the well-attested habit of mere life. The original method now enters upon a prolonged old age in which well-being has sunk into mere being. Varied freshness has been lost, and the species lives upon the blind appetitions of old usages.

The essence of Reason in its lowliest forms is its judgments upon flashes of novelty, of novelty in immediate realization and of novelty which is relevant to appetition but not yet to action. In the stabilized life there is no room for Reason. The methodology has sunk from a method of novelty into a method of repetition. Reason is the organ of emphasis upon novelty. It provides the judgment by which it passes into realization in purpose, and thence its realization in fact.

Life-tedium is fatigue derived from a thwarted urge toward novel contrast. In nature we find three ways in which stabilization is secured. They may be named: the Way of Blindness, the Way of Rhythm, the Way of Transience. These ways are not mutually exclusive. In fact the Way of Rhythm seems all-pervasive throughout life. But the Way of Blindness seems to render Transience unnecessary, and the Way of Transience diminishes the Blindness. All three ways seem to be present in a stabilized old age of mere survival, but Blindness and Transience seem to vary inversely to each other.

The Way of Blindness means relapse. This relapse eliminates those flashes of novel appetition which have constituted the means of ascent to the existing stage of complex life. These flashes are in fact part of the stage itself. They are the element of vivid novelty of enjoyment. But the ladder of ascent is now discarded. The novelties and their reasoned emphasis are excluded. The complexity attained is lived through on a lower level of operations than those which went to its attainment. The upward trend is lost. There is stabilization in some lower level, or progressive relapse. The organ of vividness, which is also the organ of novelty and the organ of fatigue, has been atrophied.

The Way of Transience means the substitution of short-lived individuals by way of protecting the species from the fatigue of the individual. Transience is really a way of blindness: it procures novel individuals to face blindly the old round of experience.

The Way of Rhythm pervades all life, and indeed all physical existence. This common principle of Rhythm is one of the reasons for believing that the root principles of life are, in some lowly form, exemplified in all types of physical existence. In the Way of Rhythm a round of experiences, forming a determinate sequence of contrasts attainable within a definite method, are codified so that the end of one such cycle is the proper antecedent stage for the beginning of another such cycle. The cycle is such that its own completion provides the conditions for its own mere repetition. It eliminates the fatigue attendant upon the repetition of any one of its parts. Only some strength of physical memory can aggregate fatigue arising from the cycle as a whole. Provided that each cycle in itself is self-repairing, the fatigue from repetition requires a high level of coordination of stretches of past experience.

At the level of human experience we do find fatigue arising from the mere repetition of cycles. The device by which this fatigue is again obviated takes the form of the preservation of the fundamental abstract structure of the cycle, combined with the variation of the concrete details of succeeding cycles. This device is particularly illustrated in music and in vision. It is of course capable of an enormous elaboration of complexity of detail. Thus the Rhythm of life is not merely to be sought in simple cyclical recurrence. The cycle element is driven into the foundation, and variations of cycles, and of cycles of cycles, are elaborated.

We find here the most obvious example of the adoption of a method. The good life is attained by the enjoyment of contrasts within the scope of the method. We exemplify in this way the action of appetition working within a framework of order. Reason finds its scope here in its function of the direction of the upward trend. In its lowliest form, Reason provides the emphasis on the conceptual clutch after some refreshing novelty. It is then Reason devoid of constructive range of abstract thought. It operates merely as the simple direct judgment lifting a conceptual flash into an effective appetition, and an effective appetition into a realized fact.

"Fatigue" is the antithesis of Reason. The operations of Fatigue constitute the defeat of Reason in its primitive character of reaching after the upward trend. Fatigue means the operation of excluding the impulse towards novelty. It excludes the opportunities of the immediate stage at which life finds itself. That stage has been reached by seizing opportunity. The meridian triumph of a method is when it facilitates opportunity without any transcending of itself. Mere repetition is the baffling of opportunity. The inertia weighing upon Reason is generation of a mere recurrent round of change, unrelieved by novelty. The urge of Reason, clogged with such inertia, is fatigue. When the baffled urge has finally vanished, life preserves its stage so far as concerns its formal operations. But it has lost the impulse by which the stage was reached, an impulse which constituted an original element in the stage itself. There has been a relapse into mere repetitive life, concerned with mere living and divested of any factor involving effort towards living well, and still less of any effort towards living better. This stage of static life never truly attains stability. It represents a slow, prolonged decay in which the complexity of the organism gradually declines towards simpler forms.

In this general description of the primitive function of Reason in animal life, the analogy of a living body, with its own self-contained organization, to the self-contained physical organization of the material universe as a whole, has been closely followed. The material universe has contained in itself, and perhaps still contains, some mysterious impulse for its energy to run upwards. This impulse is veiled from our observation, so far as concerns its general operation. But there must have been some epoch in which the dominant trend was the formation of protons, electrons, molecules, the stars. Today, so far as our observations go, they are decaying. We know more of the animal body, through the medium of our personal experience. In the animal body, we can observe the appetition towards the upward trend, with Reason as the selective agency. In the general physical universe we cannot obtain any direct knowledge of the corresponding agency by which it attained its present stage of available energy. The aggregations of energy in the form of protons, electrons, molecules, cosmic dust, stars, and planets, are there However vast may be the scale of the physical order, it appears to be finite, and it is wasting at a finite rate. However long the periods of time may have been, there must have been a beginning of the mere waste, and there must be an end to it. From nothing, there can come nothing.

The universe, as construed solely in terms of the efficient causation of purely physical interconnections, presents a sheer, insoluble contradiction. The orthodox doctrine of the physiologists demands that the operations of living bodies be explained solely in terms of the physical system of physical categories. This system within its own province, when confronted with the empirical facts, fails to include these facts apart from an act of logical suicide. The moral to be drawn from the general survey of the physical universe with its operations viewed in terms of purely physical laws, and neglected so far as they are inexpressible in such terms, is that we have omitted some general counter-agency. This counter-agency in its operation throughout the physical universe is too vast and diffusive for our direct observation. We may acquire such power as the result of some advance. But at present, as we survey the physical cosmos, there is no direct intuition of the counter-agency to which it owes its possibility of existence as a wasting finite organism.

Thus the orthodox physiological doctrine has the weakness that it rests its explanations exclusively upon the physical system, which is internally inconsistent.

In the animal body there is, as we have already seen, clear evidence of activities directed by purpose. It is therefore natural to reverse the analogy, and to argue that some lowly, diffused form of the operations of Reason constitute the vast diffused counter-agency by which the material cosmos comes into being. This conclusion amounts to the repudiation of the radical extrusion of final causation from our cosmological theory. The rejection of purpose dates from Francis Bacon at the beginning of the seventeenth century. As a methodological device it is an unquestioned success so long as we confine attention to certain limited fields.

Provided that we admit the category of final causation, we can consistently define the primary function of Reason. This function is to constitute, emphasize, and criticize the final causes and strength of aims directed towards them.

The pragmatic doctrine must accept this definition. It is obvious that pragmatism is nonsense apart from final causation. For a doctrine can never be tested unless it is acted upon. Apart from this primary function the very existence of Reason is purposeless and its origination is inexplicable. In the course of evolution why should the trend have arrived at mankind, if his activities of Reason remain without influence on his bodily actions? It is well to be quite clear on the point that Reason is inexplicable if purpose be ineffective.

Thus at the very outset the primary physiological doctrine has to be examined. This examination leads to the distinction between the authority of science in the determination of its methodology and the authority of science in the determination of the ultimate categories of explanation. We are then led to consider the natural reaction of men with a useful methodology against any evidence tending to limit the scope of that methodology. Science has always suffered from the vice of overstatement. In this way conclusions true within strict limitations have been generalized dogmatically into a fallacious universality.

This pragmatic function of Reason provides the agency procuring the upward trend of animal evolution. But the doctrine of the upward trend equally requires explanation in the purely physical cosmos. Our scientific formulation of physics displays a limited universe in process of dissipation. We require a counter-agency to explain the existence of a universe in dissipation within a finite time. The analogy of the animal body suggests that the extreme rejection of final causation from our categories of explanation has been fallacious. A satisfactory cosmology must explain the interweaving of efficient and of final causation. Such a cosmology will obviously remain an explanatory arbitrariness if our doctrine of the two modes of causation takes the form of a mere limitation of the scope of one mode by the intervention of the other mode. What we seek is such an explanation of the metaphysical nature of things that everything determinable by efficient causation is thereby determined, and that everything determinable by final causation is thereby determined. The two spheres of operation should be interwoven and required, each by the other. But neither sphere should arbitrarily limit the scope of the alternative mode.

Meanwhile, we find that the short-range function of Reason, characteristic of Ulysses, is Reason criticizing and emphasizing the subordinate purposes in nature which are the agents of final causation. This is Reason as a pragmatic agent.

In this function Reason is the practical embodiment of the urge to transform mere existence into the good existence, and to transform the good existence into the better existence.

But if we survey the universe of nature, mere static survival seems to be the general rule, accompanied by a slow decay. The instances of the upward trend are represented by a sprinkling of exceptional cases. Thus the general fact, as empirically presented to us, appears to be the upward trend of the few, combined with a slow slipping away of the old widespread physcial order forming the basis from which the ascent is made.

This empirical fact constitutes one of the deepest unsolved mysteries.

When we have recognized these two tendencies at work, it is inevitable that we ask how we can conceive the nature of things so as to include this double character. We all remember Bergson's doctrine of the *élan vital* and its relapse into matter. The double tendency of advance and relapse is here plainly stated. But we are not given any explanatory insight. The older doctrine of individual substances with their inherent qualities does not give the slightest reason for the double aspect. But there is another obvious duality in the world which it is the first business of every cosmology to consider— Body and Mind. If we follow Descartes and express this duality in terms of the concept of substance, we obtain the notion of bodily substances and of mental substances. The bodily substances have, on this theory, a vacuous existence. They are sheer facts, devoid of all intrinsic values. It is intrinsically impossible to give any reason why they should come into existence, or should endure, or should cease to exist. Descartes tells us that they are sustained by God, but fails to give any reason why God should care to do so. This conception of vacuous substantial existence lacks all explanatory insight. The movement to exclude final causation has thus ended by making the doctrine of efficient causation equally inexplicable. Descartes had to call in God, in order to push his bodies around. The two tendencies upward and downward cannot be torn apart. They exist together. Also Descartes' clean cut between bodies and mind is a misreading of the empirical facts.

We shall never elaborate an explanatory metaphysics unless we abolish this notion of valueless, vacuous existence. Vacuity is the character of an abstraction, and is wrongly introduced into the notion of a finally real thing, an actuality. Universals and propositions are vacuous, but are not actualities. But if we discard the notion of vacuous existence, we must conceive each actuality as attaining an end for itself. Its very existence

is the presentation of its many components to itself, for
the sake of its own ends. In other words, an actuality
is a complex unity, which can be analysed as a process of feeling its own components. This is the doctrine that each actuality is an occasion of experience,
the outcome of its own purposes.

Now I am pursuing the ordinary scientific method
of searching for an explanation. Having found one example of a fundamental duality in the universe, namely
the physical tendency towards degradation and the
counter-tendency upwards, I am enumerating the other
basic dualities, with the hope of tying them up into one
coherent concept in which they explain each other. We
have now to ask how we can interpret the upward and
the downward trends, and body and mind, as two co-
ordinate dualities essential in the nature of experience.

Bodily experience is sheer physical experience. Such
experience is the sheer final enjoyment of being definitely something. It is self-definition as constituting one
sheer fact among other things, namely among other
actualities and selected forms of definiteness. Physical
experience is the matter-of-fact enjoyment of just those
items which are given to that occasion. Every component in physical experience is playing its part in sheer
matter-of-fact.

But every occasion of experience is dipolar. It is mental experience integrated with physical experience. Mental experience is the converse of bodily experience. It is the experience of forms of definiteness in respect to their disconnection from any particular physical experience, but with abstract evaluation of what they *can* contribute to such experience. Consciousness is no necessary element in mental experience. The lowest form of mental experience is blind urge towards a *form of* experience, that is to say, an urge towards a *form for* realization. These forms of definiteness are the Platonic forms, the Platonic ideas, the medieval universals.

In its essence, mentality is the urge towards some vacuous definiteness, to include it in matter-of-fact which is non-vacuous enjoyment. This urge is appetition. It is emotional purpose: it is agency. Mentality is no more vacuous than is physical enjoyment. But it brings the sheer vacuity of the form into the realization of experience. In physical experience, the forms are the defining factors: in mental experience the forms connect the immediate occasions with occasions which lie beyond. The connection of immediate fact with the future resides in its appetitions.

The higher forms of intellectual experience only arise when there are complex integrations, and reintegrations, of mental and physical experience. Reason then appears as a criticism of appetitions. It is a second-order type of mentality. It is the appetition of appetitions.

Mental experience is the organ of novelty, the urge beyond. It seeks to vivify the massive physical fact, which is repetitive, with the novelties which beckon. Thus mental experience contains in itself a factor of anarchy. We can understand order, because in the recesses of our own experience there is a contrasting element which is anarchic.

But sheer anarchy means the nothingness of experience. We enjoy the contrasts of our own variety in virtue of the order which removes the incompatibility of mere diversity. Thus mental experience must itself be canalized into order.

In its lowest form, mental experience is canalized into slavish conformity. It is merely the appetition towards, or from, whatever in fact already is. The slavish thirst in a desert is mere urge from intolerable dryness. This lowest form of slavish conformity pervades all nature. It is rather a capacity for mentality, than mentality itself. But it *is* mentality. In this lowly form it evades no difficulties: it strikes out no new ways: it produces no disturbance of the repetitive character of physical fact. It can stretch out no arm to save nature from its ultimate decay. It is degraded to being merely one of the actors in the efficient causation.

But when mentality is working at a high level, it brings novelty into the appetitions of mental experience. In this function, there is a sheer element of anarchy. But mentality now becomes self-regulative. It canalizes its own operations by its own judgments. It introduces a higher appetition which discriminates among its own anarchic productions. Reason appears. It is Reason, thus conceived, which is the subject-matter of this discussion. We have to consider the introduction of anarchy, the revolt from anarchy, the use of anarchy, and the regulation of anarchy. Reason civilizes the brute force of anarchic appetition. Apart from anarchic appetition, nature is doomed to slow descent towards nothingness. Mere repetitive experience gradually eliminates element after element and fades towards vacuity. Mere anarchic appetition accomplishes quickly the same end, reached slowly by repetition. Reason is the special embodiment in us of the disciplined counter-agency which saves the world.

CHAPTER TWO

CHAPTER TWO

In the preceding chapter, two aspects of the function of Reason have been discriminated. In one aspect, the function of Reason was practical. To its operation, the piecemeal discovery and clarification of methodologies is due. In this way it not only elaborates the methodology, but also lifts into conscious experience the detailed operations possible within the limits of that method. In this aspect, Reason is the enlightenment of purpose; within limits, it renders purpose effective. Also when it has rendered purpose effective, it has fulfilled its function and lulls itself with self-satisfaction. It has finished its task. This aspect of the operations of Reason was connected with the legend of Ulysses.

The other aspect of the function of Reason was connected with the life-work of Plato. In this function Reason is enthroned above the practical tasks of the world. It is not concerned with keeping alive. It seeks with disinterested curiosity an understanding of the world. Naught that happens is alien to it. It is driven forward by the ultimate faith that all particular fact is understandable as illustrating the general principles of its own nature and of its status among other particular facts. It fulfils its function when understanding has been gained. Its sole satisfaction is that experience has been understood. It presupposes life, and seeks life rendered good with the goodness of understanding. Also so long as understanding is incomplete, it remains to that extent unsatisfied. It thus constitutes itself the urge from the good life to the better life. But the progress which it seeks is always the progress of a better understanding. This is the urge of disinterested curiosity. In this function Reason serves only itself. It is its own dominant interest, and is not deflected by motives derived from other dominant interests which it may be promoting. This is the speculative Reason.

There is a strong moral intuition that speculative understanding for its own sake is one of the ultimate elements in the good life. The passionate claim for freedom of thought is based upon it. Unlike some other moral feelings, this intuition is not widespread. Throughout the generality of mankind it flickers with very feeble intensity. But it has been transmitted through the generations in a succession of outstanding individuals who command unquestioning reverence. Also the perennial struggle between Reason and Authority, is tinged with bitterness by the intrusion of this sentiment of an ultimate moral claim.

The whole story of Solomon's dream suggests that the antithesis between the two functions of Reason is not quite so sharp as it seems at first sight. The speculative Reason produces that accumulation of theoretical understanding which at critical moments enables a transition to be made toward new methodologies. Also the discoveries of the practical understanding provide the raw material necessary for the success of the speculative Reason. But when all allowance has been made for this interplay of the two functions, there remains the essential distinction between operations of Reason governed by the purposes of some external dominant interest, and operations of Reason governed by the immediate satisfaction arising from themselves. For example, truthfulness as an element in one's own self-respect issues from a reverence for Reason in its own right. Whereas truthfulness as a dodge usually necessary for a happy life depends upon the notion of Reason as serving alien purposes. Sometimes these two grounds for truthfulness are at issue with each other. It may happen that the moral issues depending on the latter ground for immediate truthfulness, or for its abandonment, may be superior to those depending on the former ground. But the point of immediate interest is that these two grounds for truthfulness bear witness to the two functions of Reason.

The history of the practical Reason must be traced back into the animal life from which mankind emerged. Its span is measured in terms of millions of years, if we have regard to the faint sporadic flashes of intelligence which guided the slow elaboration of methods. A survey of species seems to show that a customary method soon supersedes the necessity for such flashes of progress. In this way custom supersedes any trace of thought which might transcend it. The species sinks into a stationary stage in which thought is canalized between the banks of custom.

The history of the speculative Reason is altogether shorter. It belongs to the history of civilization, and its span is about six thousand years. But the critical discovery which gave to the speculative Reason its supreme importance was made by the Greeks. Their discovery of mathematics and of logic introduced method into speculation. Reason was now armed with an objective test and with a method of progress. In this way Reason was freed from its sole dependence on mystic vision and fanciful suggestion. Its method of evolution was derived from itself. It ceased to produce a mere series of detached judgments. It produced systems instead of inspirations. The speculative Reason, armed with the Greek methods, is older than two thousand years only by a few centuries.

The ascription of the modern phase of the speculative Reason wholly to the Greeks, is an exaggeration. The great Asiatic civilizations, Indian and Chinese, also produced variants of the same method. But none of these variants gained the perfected technique of the Greek method. Their modes of handling speculative Reason were effective for the abstract religious speculation, and for philosophical speculation, but failed before natural science and mathematics. The Greeks produced the final instrument for the discipline of speculation.

If, however, we include the Asiatic anticipations, we may give about three thousand years for the effective use of speculative Reason. This short period constitutes the modern history of the human race. Within this period all the great religions have been produced, the great rational philosophies, the great sciences. The inward life of man has been transformed.

But until the last hundred and fifty years, the speculative Reason produced singularly little effect upon technology and upon art. It is arguable that on the whole within the modern period art made no progress, and in some respects declined. Having regard to the rise of modern music, we may reject the theory of a general decline in art. But, on the whole, as artists we certainly have not surpassed the men of a thousand years before Christ, and it is doubtful whether we reach their level. We seem to care less about art. Perhaps we have more to think about, and so neglect to cultivate our esthetic impulses.

Technology has certainly improved during the last three thousand years. But it would be difficult to discern any influence of the speculative Reason upon this progress, until the most recent period. There does not seem to have been much quickening of the process. For example, the technology of Europe in the eighteenth century had made a very moderate advance over that of the Roman Empire in its prime. The advance does not seem to be much greater than that made in the two thousand years preceding this culmination of the classical civilization.

The enormous advance in the technology of the last hundred and fifty years arises from the fact that the speculative and the practical Reason have at last made contact. The speculative Reason has lent its theoretic activity, and the practical Reason has lent its methodologies for dealing with the various types of facts. Both functions of Reason have gained in power. The speculative Reason has acquired content, that is to say, material for its theoretic activity to work upon, and the methodic Reason has acquired theoretic insight transcending its immediate limits. We should be on the threshold of an advance in all the values of human life.

But such optimism requires qualification. The dawn of brilliant epochs is shadowed by the massive obscurantism of human nature. Obscurantism is the inertial resistance of the practical Reason, with its millions of years behind it, to the interference with its fixed methods arising from recent habits of speculation. This obscurantism is rooted in human nature more deeply than any particular subject of interest. It is just as strong among the men of science as among the clergy, and among professional men and business men as among the other classes. Obscurantism is the refusal to speculate freely on the limitations of traditional methods. It is more than that: it is the negation of the importance of such speculation, the insistence on incidental dangers. A few generations ago the clergy, or to speak more accurately, large sections of the clergy were the standing examples of obscurantism. Today their place has been taken by scientists—

By merit raised to that bad eminence.

The obscurantists of any generation are in the main constituted by the greater part of the practitioners of the dominant methodology. Today scientific methods are dominant, and scientists are the obscurantists.

In order to understand our situation today we must note that in the sixteenth and seventeenth centuries the educated section of western Europe inherited the results of about five centuries of intense speculative activity. The mistaken expectation of obtaining a dogmatic finality in speculative first principles has obscured the very considerable success of this speculative epoch. By reason of the preservation of manuscripts to an extent enjoyed by no previous nascent civilization, this ferment of speculation could appropriate the thoughts of the earlier classical speculation, Pagan and Christian, terminating with the decadence of Rome. This advantage carried with it a weakness. The medieval movement was too learned. It formed a closed system of thinking about other people's thoughts. In this way, medieval philosophy, and indeed modern philosophy, detracted from its utility as a discipline of speculative Reason by its inadequate grasp of the fecundity of nature and of the corresponding fecundity of thought. The scholastics confined themselves to framing systems out of a narrow round of ideas. The systems were very intelligently framed. Indeed they were marvels of architectonic genius. But there are more ideas in heaven and on earth than were thought of in their philosophy.

Yet when all this concession has been made to the defects of scholasticism, its success was overwhelming. It formed the intellectual basis of one of the periods of quickest advance known to history. The comparison of the intellectual feebleness of the men, even the ablest men, of the ninth and tenth centuries with the intellectual group of the men of the thirteenth century discloses the extent of this advance. It is not merely that in the earlier times the men knew less. They were intrinsically less able in moving about among general ideas. They failed to discriminate between minor peculiarities of details and the major notions. The power of going for the penetrating idea, even if it has not yet been worked into any methodology, is what constitutes the progressive force of Reason. The great Greeks had this knack to an uncanny degree. The men of the thirteenth century had it. The men of the tenth century lacked it. In between there lay three centuries of speculative philosophy. The story is told to perfection in Henry Osborn Taylor's book, *The Mediaeval Mind*. What scholasticism gave to the European world, was penetration in the handling of ideas.

All things work between limits. This law applies even to the speculative Reason. The understanding of a civilization is the undertsanding of its limits. The penetration of the generations from the thirteenth to the seventeenth centuries worked within the limits of the ideas provided by scholasticism. These five centuries represent a period of the broadening of interests rather than a period of intellectual growth. Scholasticism had exhausted its possibilities. It had provided a capital of fundamental ideas and it had wearied mankind in its efforts to provide a final dogmatic system by the method of meditating on those ideas. New interests crept in, slowly at first and finally like an avalanche—Greek literature, Greek art, Greek mathematics, Greek science. The men of the Renaissance wore their learning more lightly than did the scholastics. They tempered it with the joy of direct experience. Thus another ancient secret was discovered, a secret never wholly lost, but sadly in the background among the learned section of the medievals,—the habit of looking for oneself, the habit of observation.

The first effect was confusion. The fourteenth and fifteenth centuries give an impression of more enlightenment, but of less intellectual power than does the thirteenth century. In some ways it suggests an intellectual throwback to the tenth century. There is the sense of dazed men groping, so far as concerns intellectual interests. The men of the early Renaissance never seem quite clear in their minds whether they should sacrifice a cock or celebrate the mass. They compromised by doing both.

But this analogy is very superficial. The medieval inheritance was never lost. After the first period of bewilderment, their penetration in the circle of scholastic ideas came to the fore. The men of the sixteenth and seventeenth centuries founded the various modern sciences, natural sciences and moral sciences, with their first principles expressed in terms which the great scholastics would have understood at a glance.

The reason why the founders of modern science were so unconscious of their debt to the medievals was that they had no idea that men could think in any other terms, or for lack of penetration could fail to think at all. Galileo and his antagonists the "Aristotelians" were rival schools employing the same general stock of ideas, and with the same penetrative ability in handling those ideas. The recasting of the medieval ideas so as to form the foundations of the modern sciences was one of the intellectual triumphs of the world. It was chiefly accomplished in the seventeenth century, though the whole process occupied about two or three centuries, taking into consideration all the sciences. But in celebrating this triumph it is ungrateful to forget the earlier centuries of scholastic preparation.

Science has been developed under the impulse of the speculative Reason, the desire for explanatory knowledge. Its reaction on technology did not commence till after the invention of the improved steam engine in the year 1769. Even then, the nineteenth century was well advanced before this reaction became one of the dominating facts. Of course, scientific instruments were invented—the telescope, the microscope, and the thermometer, for instance. Also some slight reactions on technical procedure can be traced. But the instruments were used mainly for scientific purposes, and technical improvements were initiated from hints gathered from all kinds of chances, scientific knowledge among others. There was nothing systematic and dominating in the interplay between science and technical procedure. The one great exception was the foundation of the Greenwich Observatory for the improvement of navigation.

The antagonism between science and metaphysics has, like all family quarrels, been disastrous. It was provoked by the obscurantism of the metaphysicians in the later Middle Ages. Or course, there were many exceptions. For example, the famous Cardinal, Nicholas of Cusa, illustrated the fact that quite a different turn might have been given the history of European thought. But the understanding of the proper functions of speculative thought was hampered by the fallacy of dogmatism. It was conceived that metaphysical thought started from principles which were individually clear, distinct, and certain. The result was that the tentative methods of science seemed quite at variance with dogmatic habits of metaphysicians. Also science itself was not quite so certain of its tentative procedure. The triumph of the Newtonian physics settled science upon a dogmatic foundation of materialistic ideas which lasted for two centuries. Unfortunately this approach to the metaphysical dogmatism did not produce a sense of fellowship even in evil habits. For if scientific materialism be the last word, metaphysics must be useless for physical science. The ultimate truths about nature are then not capable of any explanatory interpretation. On this theory, all that there is to be known is that inexplicable bits of matter are hurrying about with their motions correlated by inexplicable laws expressible in terms of their spatial relations to each other. If this be the final dogmatic truth, philosophy can have nothing to say to natural science.

In addition to the natural human tendency to turn a successful methodology into a dogmatic creed, the two sciences of mathematics and theology must bear the blame of fostering the dogmatic habit in European thought. The premises of mathematics seem clear, distinct, and certain. Arithmetic and geometry, as it seemed, could not be otherwise and they applied throughout the realm of nature. Also theology, by reason of its formulation of questions concerning our most intimate, sensitive interests, has always shrunk from facing the moments of bewilderment inherent in any tentative approach to the formulation of ideas.

The separation of philosophy and natural science, due to the dominance of Newtonian materialism, is indicated by the division of science into "moral science" and "natural science." For example, the University of Cambridge has inherited the term "moral science" for its department of philosophic studies. The notion is that philosophy is concerned with topics of the mind, and that natural science takes care of topics concerning matter. The whole conception of philosophy as concerned with the discipline of the speculative Reason, to which nothing is alien, has vanished. Newton himself was one of the early scientists who most emphatically repudiated the intrusion of metaphysics into science. There is plenty of evidence that, like many another man of genius, his nerves were delicately balanced. For such men the intrusion of alien considerations into the narrow way of a secure technology produces mere bewildered irritation, by reason of its disturbance of the sense of supreme mastery within the methods of their technique. Of course it would be foolish to believe that any man should dissipate his energies by straying beyond his own best lines of activity. But the pursuit of knowledge is a cooperative enterprise, and the repudiation of the relevance of diverse modes of approach to the same topic requires more justification than appeal to the limitations of individual activities.

The pathetic desire of mankind to find themselves starting from an intellectual basis which is clear, distinct, and certain, is illustrated by Newton's boast, *hypotheses non fingo*, at the same time when he enunciated his law of universal gravitation. This law states that every particle of matter attracts every other particle of matter; though at the moment of enunciation only planets and heavenly bodies had been observed to attract "particles of matter." The verification, that two particles of matter, neither of them heavenly bodies, would attract each other, had to wait for nearly a hundred years to elapse. But there was a second meaning to Newton's motto. It was an anti-Cartesian statement directed against the vortices. He was, quite correctly, pointing out that his law expressed a sheer fact, and was not accompanied by any explanatory considerations concerning the character or distribution of matter. The nemesis of the Newtonian physics was this barrier of materialism, constituting a block to any further advance to rationalism. The pragmatic value of Newton's methodology at that stage of scientific history is not in question. The interesting fact is the clutch at dogmatic finality.

I need not waste time in pointing out how the finality both of the cosmological scheme and of the particular law in question has now passed into Limbo. Newton *was* weaving hypotheses. His hypotheses speculatively embodied the truth vaguely discerned; they embodied this truth in a definite formulation which far outran the powers of analytic intuition of his age. The formulae required limitation as to the scope of their application.

This definition of scope has now been provided by recent formulae which in their turn will, in the progress of science, have their scope of application defined. Newton's formulae were not false: they were unguardedly stated. Einstein's formulae are not false: they are unguardedly stated. We now know how to guard Newton's formulae: we are ignorant of the limitations of Einstein's formulae. In scientific investigations the question, True or False?, is usually irrelevant. The important question is, In what circumstances is this formula true, and in what circumstances is it false? If the circumstances of truth be infrequent or trivial or unknown, we can say, with sufficient accuracy for daily use, that the formula is false.

Of course the unknown limitations to Einstein's formulae constitute a yet more subtle limitation to Newton's formula. In this way dogmatic finality vanishes and is replaced by an asymptotic approach to the truth.

The doctrine that science starts from clear and distinct elements in experience, and that it develops by a clear and distinct process of elaboration, dies hard. There is a constant endeavor to explain the methodology of science in terms which, by reason of their clarity and distinctness, require no metaphysical elucidation. Undoubtedly it is possible to express the procedure of science with a happy ambiguity which can receive interpretation from a variety of metaphysical schools. But when we press the question so as to determine without ambiguity the procedure of science, we become involved in the metaphysical formulations of the speculative Reason.

The modern doctrine, popular among scientists, is that science is the mere description of things observed. As such it assumes nothing, neither an objective world, nor causation, nor induction. A simple formula which describes the universals common to many occurrences is scientifically preferable to the complexity of many descriptions of many occurrences. Thus the quest of science is simplicity of description. The conclusion is that science, thus defined, needs no metaphysics. We can then revert to the naïve doctrine of the University of Cambridge, and divide knowledge into natural science and moral science, each irrelevant to the other.

This doctrine is beautifully clear; and in the sense in which the doctrine is clear, natural science can be of no importance. We can only urge the importance of science by destroying the clarity of the doctrine.

Mere observations are particular occurrences. Thus if science be concerned with mere observations, it is an epitome of certain occurrences in the lives of certain men of science. A treatise on a scientific subject is merely an alternative way of editing a *"Scientific Who's Who"* with most of the proper names left out. For science is only concerned with particular observations made by particular men. Thus the world is in possession of four kinds of biographies, the old-fashioned *"Life and Letters"* in two volumes, the new-fashioned biography of the Lytton Strachey school, the *Who's Who* type, and the variant on the *Who's Who* type which is termed a treatise on some particular branch of science. Unless we are interested in the particular observers the scientific treatise is of no interest. Unfortunately most of the observers' names are omitted in these treatises—so all interest has evaporated.

Thus, if the doctrine of science as the quest for simplicity of description, be construed in the sense in which it frees science from metaphysics, in that sense science loses its importance. But, as the doctrine is usually handled by its adherents, metaphysics having been dismissed by one interpretation, the importance of science is preserved by the substitution of another interpretation. Two new notions are introduced, both requiring metaphysical discussion for their elucidation. One is the notion of inductive generalization, whereby future observations are brought into the scope of the scientific statements. The other is a more complex notion. It commences by introducing the notion of the observable, but not observed. It then proceeds by introducing a speculative description of spatio-temporal occurrences which constitute the factual basis in virtue of which this observability is predicated. It finally proceeds to predict, on the basis of this description and by reason of the facts thus described, the observability of occurrences generically different from any hitherto made.

For example, one type of observation, wholly visual, suggests a theory of electromagnetic equations. By the aid of this theory the design of radio apparatus, transmitting and receiving, is worked out. Finally a band plays in the laboratory of some radio station and people over an area with a radius of hundreds of miles listen to the music. Is it credible to believe that the only principle involved is the mere description of the original particular observations?

We are told, however, that we have misconstrued the intermediate step by terming it "a speculative description of spatio-temporal occurrences." The proper way of expressing the procedure of science is to say that the intermediate step is simply the production of a mathematical formula, and that by the aid of this formula the experiences of the people with receiving sets are predicted. But what is the formula doing? It may have some relevance to the sequence of experiences in some scientist's mind, expressing the transition from his original visual experiences to his final enjoyment of an excellent band. The doctrine seems unlikely and far-fetched. By a stretch of the mind, I can imagine it. But we have got to account for the experiences of the unlearned multitude with radio sets. They are ignorant of the original experiments, ignorant of the whereabouts of the band and of the radio laboratory, and ignorant of the inside mechanism both of the generating station and of their own radio sets. What on earth has the *mere* mathematical formula to do with the experiences of this multitude of listeners, endowed with this comprehensive ignorance and taking their rest after good dinners and a hard day's work?

Is the formula a magical incantation? We can parallel this modern doctrine of the mere description of observations together with the intervention of a mere formula, by recalling our memories of childhood. There is a large audience, a magician comes upon the stage, places a table in front of him, takes off his coat, turns it inside out, shows himself to us, then commences voluble patter with elaborate gestures, and finally produces two rabbits from his hat. We are asked to believe that it was the patter that did it.

The common sense of the matter is, that the mathematical formulae are descriptive of those characteristics of the common external world which are relevant to the transmission of physical states from the band to the bodies of the listeners.

If this be true, we are now a long way from the sweet simplicity of the original doctrine. We have introduced the notion of the external world with its spatio-temporal occurrences, speculatively described by science. We have introduced the notion of potentiality, by substituting the word "observable" for the word "observed." Also hundreds of millions of dollars have been risked in reliance upon inductive generalization. If we ask what we mean by all this apparatus of vague notions, our only appeal must be to the speculative Reason.

It is quite true that exactly at this point we can damp down any further speculative Reason, and can relapse into the routine of successful methodology. But the claim of science that it can produce an understanding of its procedures within the limits of its own categories, or that those categories themselves are understandable without reference to their status within the widest cate-

gories under exploration by the speculative Reason—
that claim is entirely unfounded. Insofar as philosophers
have failed, scientists do not know what they are talk-
ing about when they pursue their own methods; and
insofar as philosophers have succeeded, to that extent
scientists can attain an understanding of science. With
the success of philosophy, blind habits of scientific
thought are transformed into analytic explanation.

The Cartesian dualism, whereby the final actualities
were divided into bodies and minds, and the Newtonian
materialistic cosmology, combined to set a false goal
before philosophic speculation. The notion of mere
bodies and of mere minds was accepted uncritically.
But the ideal of explaining either minds in terms of
bodies, or bodies in terms of minds guided speculative
thought. First Hobbes made bodies fundamental, and
reduced minds to derivative factors. Then Berkeley
made minds fundamental, and reduced bodies to derivative factors—mere ideas in the minds, and more
particularly in the mind of God. The most important
effect on the relations of philosophy to natural science
was, however, produced neither by Hobbes nor by
Berkeley, but by Kant. The effect of his *Critique of
Pure Reason* was to reduce the system of nature to mere
appearance—or, to use the Greek word, the order of

nature is phenomenal. But whether we prefer the word "appearance," or the word "phenomenon," the effect is the same. There can be no metaphysics of nature, and no approach to metaphysics by scanning the order of nature. For nature is a mere derivative appearance; and when we consider it, we are remote trom any intuition which tells of final truths. It is true that Kant himself did not draw that conclusion. The starry heavens affected him, a triumph of the obvious over philosophy. But in the long run, the effect of the Kantian point of view was to degrade science to the consideration of derivative details. But again the obvious triumphed. There is an insistent importance in the details of our phenomenal life in the phenomenal world. Kant denied that this phenomenal system could bring us to metaphysics. Yet obviously here we are, living phenomenally among phenomena. August Comte was the nemesis which issued from the *Critique of Pure Reason*. The positivist position inverts the Kantian argument. Positivism holds that we are certainly in the world, and it also holds with Kant that the system of the world reflects no light upon metaphysics. Anyhow from the side of philosophy, Kant drove a wedge between science and the speculative Reason. This issue from Kant did not obtain its proper development till the nineteenth century. Kant himself and his immediate followers were intensely interested in natural science. But the English neo-Kantians and neo-Hegelians of the mid-nineteenth century were remote from natural science.

This antagonism between philosophy and natural science has produced unfortunate limitations of thought on both sides. Philosophy has ceased to claim its proper generality, and natural science is content with the narrow round of its methods. The seventeenth century had built the categoreal notions of the sciences so firmly that the divorce from philosophy practically had no effect on immediate progress. We have now come to a critical period of the general reorganisation of categories of scientific thought. Also sciences, such as psychology and physiology, are hovering on the edge of the crevasse separating science from philosophy.

The obscurantist attitude of science is likely to be disastrous in retarding progress. It may be that we are not yet ready to effect a closer union between speculative thought and scientific method. One thing is certain: scientific opinion can have no possible justification for coming to this conclusion. The rejection of any source of evidence is always treason to that ultimate rationalism which urges forward science and philosophy alike.

CHAPTER THREE

CHAPTER THREE

The speculative Reason is in its essence untrammelled by method. Its function is to pierce into the general reasons beyond limited reasons, to understand all methods as coordinated in a nature of things only to be grasped by transcending all method. This infinite ideal is never to be attained by the bounded intelligence of mankind. But what distinguishes men from the animals, some humans from other humans, is the inclusion in their natures, waveringly and dimly, of a disturbing element, which is the flight after the unattainable. This element is that touch of infinity which has goaded races onward, sometimes to their destruction. It is a tropism to the beckoning light—to the sun passing toward the finality of things, and to the sun arising from their origin. The speculative Reason turns east and west, to the source and to the end, alike hidden below the rim of the world.

Reason which is methodic is content to limit itself

within the bounds of a successful method. It works in the secure daylight of traditional practical activity. It is the discipline of shrewdness. Reason which is speculative questions the methods, refusing to let them rest. The passionate demand for freedom of thought is a tribute to the deep connection of the speculative Reason with religious intuitions. The Stoics emphasized this right of the religious spirit to face the infinitude of things, with such understanding as it might. In the first period when the speculative Reason emerged as a distinguishable force, it appeared in the guise of sporadic inspirations. Seers, prophets, men with a new secret, appeared. They brought to the world fire, or salvation, or release, or moral insight. Their common character was to be bearers of some imaginative novelty, relevant and yet transcending traditional ways.

The real importance of the Greeks for the progress of the world is that they discovered the almost incredible secret that the speculative Reason was itself subject to orderly method. They robbed it of its anarchic character without destroying its function of reaching beyond set bounds. That is why we now speak of the speculative Reason in the place of Inspiration. Reason appeals to the orderliness of what is reasonable while "speculation" expresses the transcendence of any particular method. The Greek secret is, how to be bounded by method even in its transcendence. They hardly understand their own discovery. But we have the advantage of having watched it in operation for twenty centuries.

The world's experience of professed seers has on the whole been very unfortunate. In the main, they are a shady lot with a bad reputation. Even if we put aside those with some tinge of insincerity, there still remain the presumptuous, ignorant, incompetent, unbalanced band of false prophets who deceive the people. On the whole, the odds are so heavily against any particular prophet that, apart from some method of testing, perhaps it is safer to stone them, in some merciful way. The Greeks invented logic in the broadest sense of that term—the logic of discovery. The Greek logic as finally perfected by the experience of centuries provides a set of criteria to which the content of a belief should be subjected. These are:

  (i) Conformity to intuitive experience:

 (ii) Clarity of the propositional content:

(iii) Internal Logical consistency:

(iv) External Logical consistency:

 (v) Status of a *Logical* scheme with,

    (a) widespread conformity to experience,

(b) no discordance with experience,

(c) coherence among its categoreal notions,

(d) methodological consequences.

The misconception which has haunted the ages of thought down to the present time is that these criteria are easy to apply. For example, the Greek and the medieval thinkers were under the impression that they could easily obtain clear and distinct premises which conformed to experience. Accordingly they were comparatively careless in the criticism of premises, and devoted themselves to the elaboration of deductive systems. The moderns have, equally with the Greeks, assumed that it is easy to formulate exactly expressed propositions. They have also assumed that the interrogation of experience is a straightforward operation. But they have recognized that the main effort is to be devoted to the discovery of propositions which do in fact conform to experience. Thus the moderns stress induction. The view which I am maintaining is that none of these operations are easy. In fact they are extremely difficult. Apart from a complete metaphysical understanding of the universe, it is very difficult to understand any proposition clearly and distinctly, so far as concerns the analysis of its component elements.

Again the analysis of experience without the introduction of interpretive elements which may be faulty, is extremely difficult. It follows also from these two difficulties that judgment of direct conformity to experience is very difficult to bring to a decisive issue, with the elimination of all elements of doubt.

There is also some doubt even as to the self-consistency of a proposition. For if the analysis of the proposition be vague, there is always a possibility that a more complete analysis will disclose a flaw. The same doubt also applies to the fourth criterion which is that of external consistency. In this case we are comparing the proposition under the scrutiny with other propositions accepted as true.

It is obvious that if the first two criteria were capable of easy determination nothing else would be wanted. Also if the first four could be decisively determined, the fifth criterion would be unnecessary. But this last criterion is evidently a procedure, to remedy the difficulty of judging individual propositions, by having recourse to a system of ideas, whose mutual relevance shall lend to each other clarity, and which hang together so that the verification of some reflects upon the verification of the others. Also if the system has the character of suggesting methodologies of which it is explanatory, it gains the character of generating ideas coherent with itself and receiving continuous verification.

The whole point of the fifth criterion is that the scheme produces a greater understanding of the world, including the better definition of ideas and the more direct analysis of immediate fact. A single proposition rests upon vague apprehensions: whereas a scheme of ideas provides its own measure of definiteness by the mutual relatedness of its own categoreal methods.

It is by their emphasis of schemes of thought that the Greeks founded the various branches of science, which have remade civilization. A proposition which falls within a scientific scheme is accepted with surprisingly slight direct verification. For example, at the present time we all accept the famous doctrine of the shift of the spectral lines. But so far as direct evidence is concerned, there are some experiments on rays from the sun, with very dubious interpretations, and the clearcut instance of the light from the dark companion of Sirius. There are millions of untested stars, apart from the question as to whether the same star will always give the same effect. But no one doubts the doctrine because it falls within the reigning scientific scheme. The importance of the scheme is illustrated by imagining some occurrence which does not fall within any scheme. You go to a strange foreign country, and among your first observations on your first day is that of a man standing on his head. If you are cautious, you will refrain from generalizing on the propensity of the inhabitants to stand on their heads; also half your friends will disbelieve you when you mention the incident. Yet your direct evidence is comparable to that respecting the shift of the spectral lines.

The production of a scheme is a major effort of the speculative Reason. It involves imagination far outrunning the direct observations. The interwoven group of categoreal notions which constitute the scheme allow of derivative extension by the constructive power of deductive logic. Throughout the whole range of these propositions respecting the interrelations of the forms of things, some of them allow of direct comparison with experience. The extent of its conformity or non-conformity with observed fact can thus be explored. A scheme which, for a time at least, is useless methodologically, is one which fails to yield these observable contacts with fact.

An abstract scheme which is merely developed by the abstract methodology of logic, and which fails to achieve contact with fact by means of a correlate practical methodology of experiment, may yet be of the utmost importance. The history of modern civilization shows that such schemes fulfil the promise of the dream of Solomon. They first amplify life by satisfying the peculiar claim of the speculative Reason, which is understanding for its own sake. Secondly, they represent the capital of ideas which each age holds in trust for its successors. The ultimate moral claim that civilization lays upon its possessors is that they transmit, and add to, this reserve of potential development by which it has profited. One main law which underlies modern progress is that, except for the rarest accidents of chance, thought precedes observation. It may not decide the details, but it suggests the type. Nobody would count, whose mind was vacant of the idea of number. Nobody directs attention when there is nothing that he expects to see. The novel observation which comes by chance is a rare accident, and is usually wasted. For if there be no scheme to fit it into, its significance is lost. The way of thoughtless nature is by waste—a million seeds, and one tree; a million eggs, and one fish. In the same way, from a million observations of fact beyond the routine of human life it rarely happens that one useful development issues.

The comparative stagnation of Asiatic civilization after its brilliant development was due to the fact that it had exhausted its capital of ideas, the product of curiosity. Asia had no large schemes of abstract thought, energizing in the minds of men and waiting to give significance to their chance experiences. It remained in contemplation and the ideas became static. This sheer contemplation of abstract ideas had stifled the anarchic curiosity producing novelty. Speculation had faded out of Reason. Millions had seen apples fall from trees, but Newton had in his mind the mathematical scheme of dynamic relations: millions had seen lamps swinging in temples and churches, but Galileo had in his mind his vaguer anticipation of this same mathematical scheme: millions had seen animals preying on each other, vegetables choking each other, millions had endured famine and thirst, but Charles Darwin had in his mind the Malthusian scheme. The secret of progress is the speculative interest in abstract schemes of morphology. It is hardly realized for how long a time such abstract schemes can grow in the minds of men before contact with practical interests. The story of the development of mathematical physics has been told and retold, but its moral is so overwhelming that it must never be allowed out of sight.

Consider the early stages of mathematics—a few technological dodges in Egypt about two thousand years before Christ. It was a minor element in a great civilization. About five hundred years before Christ, the Greeks initiated its theoretical development for the love of the theory. This was about four or five hundred after the date of Solomon's dream, the greatest prophecy ever made. The genius of the Greeks was shown by their clear divination of the importance of mathematics for the study of nature. The necessity for fostering the development of abstract morphology is illustrated by considering the state of the science of geometry at the commencement of the sixteenth century. The science had been studied for about two thousand years. It had been elaborated in great detail. But, allowing for some minor qualifications, nothing had come from it except the intrinsic interest of the study. Then, as if a door had suddenly opened, Kepler produced the first important utilization of conic sections, the first among hundreds, Descartes and Desargues revolutionized the methods of the science, Newton wrote his *Principia*, and the modern period of civilization commenced. Apart from the capital of abstract ideas which had accumulated slowly during two thousand years, our modern life would have been impossible. There is nothing magical about mathematics as such. It is simply the greatest example of a science of abstract forms.

The abstract theory of music is another such science: the abstract theory of political economy is another: and the abstract theory of the currency is another. The point is that the development of abstract theory precedes the understanding of fact. The instance of political economy illustrates another important point. We all know that abstract political economy has in recent years been somewhat under a cloud. It deals with men under an abstraction; it limits its view to the "economic man." It also makes assumptions as to markets and competition which neglect many important factors. We have here an example of the necessity of transcending a given morphological scheme. Up to a point the scheme is invaluable. It clarifies thought, it suggests observation, it explains fact. But there is a strict limit to the utility of any finite scheme. If the scheme be pressed beyond its proper scope, definite error results. The art of the speculative Reason consists quite as much in the transcendence of schemes as in their utilization.

Mathematical physics suggests another reflection. We must dwell upon the extreme abstractness of the mathematical ideas involved. It is surprising that a scheme of such abstract ideas should have proved to be of such importance. We can imagine that an Egyptian country gentleman at the beginning of the Greek period might

have tolerated the technical devices of his land survey-
ors, but would have felt that the airy generalizations of
the speculative Greeks were tenuous, unpractical, and a
waste of time. The obscurantists of all ages exhibit the
same principles. All common sense is with them. Their
only serious antagonist is History, and the history of
Europe is dead against them. Abstract speculation has
been the salvation of the world—speculation which made
systems and then transcended them, speculations which
ventured to the furthest limit of abstraction. To set
limits to speculation is treason to the future.

But the weaving itself requires discipline. It has to
be kept in some relation to the general facts of this
epoch. Cosmology is the effort to frame a scheme of
the general character of the present stage of the universe. The cosmological scheme should present the
genus, for which the special schemes of the sciences
are the species. The task of Cosmology is twofold.
It restrains the aberrations of the mere undisciplined
imagination. A special scheme should either fit in with
the general cosmology, or should by its conformity to
fact present reasons why the cosmology should be
modified. In the case of such a misfit, the more probable
result is some modification of the cosmology and some

modification of the scheme in question. Thus the cosmology and the schemes of the sciences are mutually critics of each other. The limited morphology of a special science is confessedly incapable of expressing in its own categoreal notions all forms which are illustrated in the world. But it is the business of a cosmology to be adequate. For this reason a cosmology must consider those factors which have not been adequately embraced in some science. It has also to include all the sciences.

The dim recesses of experience present immense difficulties for analysis. The mere interrogation of immediate consciousness at one immediate moment tells us very little. Analytic power vanishes under such direct scrutiny. We have recourse to memory, to the testimony of others including their memories, to language in the form of the analysis of words and phrases—that is to say, to etymology and syntax. We should also consider the institutions of mankind in the light of an embodiment of their stable experience.

In the search for categorical notions sufficiently general to figure in a cosmological morphology, we must lay stress on those factors in experience which are "stable." By this it is meant that the discerning of them as illustrated in fact is not confined to a few special people, or a few special occasions. The illustration must rest on broad, widespread testimony.

Here a distinction must be made. The first discernment may be due to an exceptional man in an exceptional moment. But a secret which cannot be shared, must remain a secret. The categoreal forms should come to us with some evidence that they are widsepread in experience. But we are now considering the main difficulty of the speculative Reason, its confrontation with experience.

There is a conventional view of experience, never admitted when explicitly challenged, but persistently lurking in the tacit presuppositions. This view conceives conscious experience as a clear-cut knowledge of clear-cut items with clear-cut connections with each other. This is the conception of a trim, tidy, finite experience uniformly illuminated. No notion could be further from the truth. In the first place the equating of experience with clarity of knowledge is against evidence. In our own lives, and at any one moment, there is a focus of attention, a few items in clarity of awareness, but interconnected vaguely and yet insistently with other items in dim apprehension, and this dimness shading off imperceptibly into undiscriminated feeling.

Further, the clarity cannot be segregated from the vagueness. The togetherness of the things that are clear refuses to yield its secret to clear analytic intuition. The whole forms a system, but when we set out to describe the system direct intuition plays us false. Our conscious awareness is fluctuating, flitting, and not under control. It lacks penetration. The penetration of intuition follows upon the expectation of thought. This is the secret of attention.

But besides this character of an immediate moment of experience, these moments differ among themselves in the life of any one of us. We are alert, or we are drowsy, or we are excited, or we are contemplative, or we are asleep, or we are dreaming, or we are intently expecting, or we are devoid of any concentrated expectation. Our variety of phases is infinite.

Again when we consider other humans, and animals, an analogous variation suggests itself between their average states, and between the highest stages respectively possible for different individuals. As we descend the scale, it seems that we find in the lower types a dim unconscious drowse, of undiscriminated feeling. For the lower types, experience loses its illustration of forms, and its illumination by consciousness, and its discrimination of purpose. It seems finally to end in a massive unconscious urge derived from undiscriminated feeling, this feeling being itself a derivation from the immediate past.

The basis of all authority is the supremacy of fact over thought. Yet this contrast of fact and thought can be conceived fallaciously. For thought is a factor in the fact of experience. Thus the immediate fact is what it is, partly by reason of the thought involved in it. The quality of an act of experience is largely determined by the factor of the thinking which it contains. But the thought involved in any one such act involves an analytic survey of experience beyond itself. The supremacy of fact over thought means that even the utmost flight of speculative thought should have its measure of truth. It may be the truth of art. But thought irrelevant to the wide world of experience, is unproductive.

The proper satisfaction to be derived from speculative thought is elucidation. It is for this reason that fact is supreme over thought. This supremacy is the basis of authority. We scan the world to find evidence for this elucidatory power.

Thus the supreme verification of the speculative flight is that it issues in the establishment of a practical technique for well-attested ends, and that the speculative system maintains itself as the elucidation of that technique. In this way there is the progress from thought to practice, and regress from practice to the same thought. This interplay of thought and practice is the supreme authority. It is the test by which the charlatanism of speculation is restrained.

In human history, a practical technique embodies itself in established institutions—professional associations, scientific associations, business associations, universities, churches, governments. Thus the study of the ideas which underlie the sociological structure is an appeal to the supreme authority. It is the Stoic appeal to the "voice of nature."

But even this supreme authority fails to be final, and this for two reasons. In the first place the evidence is confused, ambiguous, and contradictory. In the second place, if at any period of human history it had been accepted as final, all progress would have been stopped. The horrid practices of the past, brutish and nasty, would have been fastened upon us for all ages. Nor can we accept the present age as our final standard. We can live, and we can live well. But we feel the urge of the trend upwards: we still look toward the better life.

We have to seek for a discipline of the speculative Reason. It is of the essence of such speculation that it transcends immediate fact. Its business is to make thought creative of the future. It effects this by its vision of systems of ideas, including observation but generalized beyond it. The need of discipline arises because the history of speculation is analogous to the history of practice. If we survey mankind, their speculations have been foolish, brutish, and nasty. The true use of history is that we extract from it general principles as to the discipline of practice and the discipline of speculation.

The object of this discipline is not stability but progress. It has been urged in these pages, that there is no true stability. What looks like stability is a relatively slow process of atrophied decay. The stable universe is slipping away from under us. Our aim is upwards.

The men who made speculation effective were the Greek thinkers. We owe to them the progressive European civilization. It is therefore common sense to observe the methods which they introduced into the conduct of thought.

In the first place, they were unboundedly curious. They probed into everything, questioned everything, and sought to understand everything. This is merely to say that they were speculative to a superlative degree. In the second place, they were rigidly systematic both in their aim at clear definition and at logical consistency. In fact, they invented logic in order to be consistent. Thirdly, they were omnivorous in their interests— natural science, ethics, mathematics, political philosophy, metaphysics, theology, esthetics, and all alike attracted their curiosity. Nor did they keep these subjects rigidly apart. They very deliberately strove to combine them into one coherent system of ideas. Fourthly, they sought truths of the highest generality. Also in seeking these truths, they paid attention to the whole body of their varied interests. Fifthly, they were men with active practical interests. Plato went to Sicily in order to assist in a political experiment, and throughout his life studied mathematics. In those days mathematics and its applications were not so separated as they can be today. No doubt, the sort of facts that he observed were the applications of mathematical theory. But no one had a keener appreciation than Plato of the divergence between the exactness of abstract thought and the vague margin of ambiguity which haunts all observation. Indeed in this respect Plato, the abstract thinker, far surpasses John Stuart Mill, the inductive philosopher. Mill in his account of the inductive methods of science never faces the difficulty that no observation ever does exactly verify the law which it is presumed to support.

Plato's feeling for the inexactness of physical experience in contrast to the exactness of thought certainly suggests that he could look for himself. Mill's determinism is, according to his own theory, an induction respecting the exactness of conformation to the conditions set by antecedent circumstances. But no one has ever had any such experience of exact conformation. No observational basis whatsoever can ever be obtained for the support of Mill's doctrine. Plato knew this primary fact about experience, Mill did not. Determinism may be the true doctrine, but it can never be proved by the methods prescribed by English empiricism.

When we come to Aristotle the enumeration of his practical activities makes us wonder that he had any time for thought at all. He analyzed the constitutions of the leading Greek states, he dissected the great dramatic literature of his age, he dissected fishes, he dissected sentences and arguments, he taught the youthful Alexander. A man, who had done these things and others, might well have been excused if he had pleaded lack of time for mere abstract thought.

In considering the culmination of Greek speculation in Plato and Aristotle the characteristics which finally stand out are the universality of their interests, the systematic exactness at which they aimed, and the generality of their thoughts. It is no rash induction to conclude that these combined characteristics constitute one main preservative of speculation from folly.

The speculative Reason works in two ways so as to submit itself to the authority of facts without loss of its mission to transcend the existing analysis of facts. In one way it accepts the limitations of a special topic, such as a science or a practical methodology. It then seeks speculatively to enlarge and recast the categoreal ideas within the limits of that topic. This is speculative Reason in its closest alliance with the methodological Reason.

In the other way, it seeks to build a cosmology expressing the general nature of the world as disclosed in human interests. It has already been pointed out, that in order to keep such a cosmology in contact with reality account must be taken of the welter of established institutions constituting the structures of human society throughout the ages. It is only in this way that we can appeal to the widespread effective elements in the experience of mankind. What those institutions stood for in the experience of their contemporaries, represents the massive facts of ultimate authority.

The discordance at once disclosed among the beliefs and purposes of men is commonplace. But in a way, the task is simplified. The superficial details at once disclose themselves by the discordance which they disclose. The concordance in general notions stands out. The very fact of institutions to effect purposes witnesses to unquestioned belief that foresight and purpose can shape the attainment of ends. The discordance over moral codes witnesses to the fact of moral experience. You cannot quarrel about unknown elements. The basis of every discord is some common experience, discordantly realized.

A cosmology should above all things be adequate. It should not confine itself to the categoreal notions of one science, and explain away everything which will not fit in. Its business is not to refuse experience but to find the most general interpretive system. Also it is not a mere juxtaposition of the various sciences. It generalizes beyond any special science, and thus provides the interpretive system which expresses their interconnection. Cosmology, since it is the outcome of the highest generality of speculation, is the critic of all speculation inferior to itself in generality.

But cosmology shares the imperfections of all the efforts of finite intelligence. The special sciences fall short of their aim, and cosmology equally fails. Thus when the novel speculation is produced a threefold problem is set. Some special science, the cosmological scheme, and the novel concept will have points of agreement and points of variance. Reason intervenes in the capacity of arbiter and yet with a further exercise of speculation. The science is modified, the cosmological outlook is modified, and the novel concept is modified. The joint discipline has eliminated elements of folly, or of mere omission, from all three. The purposes of mankind receive the consequential modification, and the shock is transmitted through the whole sociological structure of technical methods and of institutions.

Every construction of human intelligence is more special, more limited than was its originial aim. Cosmology sets out to be made from all subordinate details. Thus there should be one cosmology presiding over many sciences. Unfortunately this ideal has not been realized. The cosmological outlooks of different schools of philosophy differ. They do more than differ, they are largely inconsistent with each other. The discredit of philosophy has largely arisen from this warring of the schools.

So long as the dogmatic fallacy infests the world, this discordance will continue to be misinterpreted. If philosophy be erected upon clear and distinct ideas, then the discord of philosophers, competent and sincere men, implies that they are pursuing a will-o'-the-wisp. But as soon as the true function of rationalism is understood, that it is a gradual approach to ideas of clarity and generality, the discord is what may be expected.

The various cosmologies have in various degrees failed to achieve the generality and the clarity at which they aim. They are inadequate, vague, and push special notions beyond the proper limits of their application. For example, Descartes is obviously right, in some sense or other, when he says that we have bodies and that we have minds, and that they can be studied in some disconnection. It is what we do daily in practical life. This philosophy makes a large generalization which obviously has some important validity. But if you turn it into a final cosmology, errors will creep in. The same is true of other schools of philosophy. They all say something which is importantly true. Some types of philosophy have produced more penetrating cosmologies than other schools. At certain epochs a cosmology may be produced which includes its predecessors and assigns to them their scope of validity. But at length, that cosmology will be found out. Rivals will appear correcting it, and perhaps failing to include some of its general truths.

In this way mankind stumbles on in its task of understanding the world.

In conclusion we must recur to our initial question, which is the title of this discussion, The Function of Reason. If we survey the world as a physical system determined by its antecedent states, it presents to us the spectacle of a finite system steadily running down— losing its activities and its varieties. The various evolutionary formulae give no hint of any contrary tendency. The struggle for existence gives no hint why there should be cities. Again the crowding of houses is no explanation why houses should be beautiful. But there is in nature some tendency upwards, in a contrary direction to the aspect of physical decay. In our experience we find appetition, effecting a final causation towards ideal ends which lie outside the mere physical tendency. In the burning desert there is appetition towards water, whereas the physical tendency is towards increased dryness of the animal body. The appetition towards esthetic satisfaction by some enjoyment of beauty is equally outside the mere physical order.

But mere blind appetition would be the product of chance and could lead nowhere. In our experience, we find Reason and speculative imagination. There is a discrimination of appetitions according to a rule of fitness. This reign of Reason is vacillating, vague, and dim. But it is there.

We have thus some knowledge, in a form specialized to the special aptitudes of human beings,—we have some knowledge of that counter-tendency which converts the decay of one order into the birth of its successor.